What Is a Share of Stock?

The Basic Investor's Library

Chelsea House Publishers

What Is a Share of Stock?

JEFFREY B. LITTLE

Paul A. Samuelson
Senior Editorial Consultant

CHELSEA HOUSE PUBLISHERS   New York   Philadelphia

Editor-in-Chief Nancy Toff
Executive Editor Remmel T. Nunn
Managing Editor Karyn Gullen Browne
Copy Chief Juliann Barbato
Picture Editor Adrian G. Allen
Art Director Giannella Garrett
Manufacturing Manager Gerald Levine

Staff for WHAT IS A SHARE OF STOCK?
Senior Editor Marjorie P. K. Weiser
Associate Editor Andrea E. Reynolds
Copyeditors Gillian Bucky, Sean Dolan, Michael Goodman, Ellen Scordato
Associate Picture Editor Juliette Dickstein
Picture Researcher Cheryl Moch
Senior Designer Laurie Jewell
Designers Barbara Bachman, Jairo Botero, Laurence Ian Burns
Production Coordinator Laura McCormick

Creative Director Harold Steinberg

Contributing Editor Robert W. Wrubel
Consulting Editor Shawn Patrick Burke

3 5 7 9 8 6 4
Library of Congress Cataloging in Publication Data

Little, Jeffrey B.   What is a share of stock?

   (The Basic investor's library)
   Bibliography: p.
   Includes index.
   1. Stocks—Juvenile literature.   2. Business enterprises—Finance—Juvenile literature.
[1. Stocks. 2. Business]   I. Title.   II. Series.
HG4521.L736   1987   332.64′22   87-13788
ISBN 1-555-46-620-6
     0-7910-0323-X (pbk.)

CONTENTS

Learning the Tools of Investing

PAUL A. SAMUELSON

When asked why the great financial house of Morgan had been so successful, J. Pierpont Morgan replied, "Do you suppose that's because we take money seriously?"

Managing our personal finances is a serious business, and something we all must learn to do. We begin life dependent on someone else's income and capital. But after we become independent, it is a remorseless fact of nature that we must not only support ourselves for the present but must also start saving money for retirement. The best theory of saving that economists have is built upon this model of *life-cycle saving*: You must provide in the long years of prime working life for what modern medicine has lengthened to, potentially, decades of retirement. This life-cycle model won a 1985 Nobel Prize for my MIT colleague Franco Modigliani, and it points up the need to learn the rudiments of personal finance.

Learning to acquire wealth, however, is only part of the story. We must also learn to avoid losing what we have acquired. There is an old saying that "life insurance is *sold*, not bought." The same goes for stocks and bonds. In each case, the broker is guaranteed a profit, whether or not the customer benefits from the transaction. Knowledge is the customer's only true ally in the world of finance. Some gullible victims have lost their lifetime savings to unscrupulous sales promoters. One chap buys the Brooklyn Bridge. Another believes a stranger who asserts that gold will quickly double in price, with no risk of a drop in value. Such "con" (confidence) rackets get written up in the newspapers and on the police blotters every day.

I am concerned, however, about something less dramatic than con artists; something that is not at all illegal, but that costs ordinary citizens a thousand times more than outright embezzlement or fraud. Consider two families, neighbors who could be found in any town. They started alike. Each worked equally hard, and had about the same income. But the Smiths have to make do with half of what the Joneses have in retirement income, for one simple reason: The Joneses followed prudent practice as savers and investors, while the Smiths tried to make a killing and constantly bought and sold stocks at high commissions.

The point is, it does matter to learn how financial markets work, and how you can participate in them to your best advantage. It is important to know the difference between *common* and *preferred* stocks, between *convertible* and *zero-coupon* bonds. It is not difficult to find out what *mutual funds* are, and to understand the difference between the successful Fund A, which charges no commission, or "load," and the equally successful Fund B, which does charge the buyer such a fee.

All investing involves risk. When I was a young assistant professor, I said primly to my great Harvard teacher, Joseph Schumpeter: "We should speculate only with money we can afford to lose." He gently corrected me: "Paul, there is no such money. Besides, a speculator is merely an investor who has lost." Did Schumpeter exaggerate? Of course he did, but in the good cause of establishing the basic point of financial management: Good past performance is no guarantee of the future.

That is why *diversification* is the golden rule. "Don't put all your eggs in one basket. And watch all those baskets!" However, diversification does not mean throwing random darts at the financial pages of the newspaper to choose the best stocks in which to invest. The most diversified strategy of all would be to invest in a portfolio containing all the stocks in the comprehensive Standard & Poor's 500 Stock Index. But rather than throw random darts at the financial pages to pick out a few stocks, why not throw a large bath towel at the newspaper instead? Buy a bit of everything in proportion to its value in the larger world: Buy more General Motors than Ford, because GM is the bigger company; buy General Electric as well as GM because the auto industry is just one of many industries. That is called being an *index investor*. Index investing makes sense because 70 out of 100 investors who try to do better than the Standard & Poor's 500, the sober record shows, do worse over a 30-year period.

Do not take my word for this. The second lesson in finance is to be skeptical of what writers and other experts say, and that includes being skeptical of professors of economics. So I wish readers *Bon voyage!* on their cruise to command the fundamentals of investing. On your mainship flag, replace the motto "Nothing ventured, nothing gained" with the Latin words *Caveat emptor*—Let the buyer beware.

What Is a Share of Stock?

Every business day, the evening news or your daily paper reports on the progress of the stock market: "Market Up 23 Points!" "Dow Climbs to Record High!" or "Market Plunges to Low for Year!" What does it all mean, and why is it so important?

The stock market is where people buy and sell shares of stocks. Each share of stock represents a part ownership in a company. Every hour that the stock exchange is open, people are buying and selling parts of the companies that produce the products and services we use every day: McDonald's, General Motors, Quaker Oats, Sears Roebuck, Black & Decker. These companies and hundreds of others each have millions of shares of stock that trade every business day on the floor of the U.S. stock exchange.

9

How do shares of stock originate? How are their prices determined? For shares to be traded from one owner to another, a company must first be created. How does the company begin, and where does the money come from?

This book will explain how a company is born, how its shares of stock are created, and the way in which those shares are priced. You will be introduced to Charlie and follow him as he founds the New-Design Chair Company, typical of the many enterprises that are launched almost daily. You will also see the basics of our economic system at work. Our economic system is an efficient way for a society to create new products, employ large numbers of motivated workers, and respond to the needs of consumers. This type of economic system is known as capitalism. *Capital* is the money used to create new businesses or expand older ones. It is the "seed money" that ultimately provides us with the products and services we use regularly.

THE NEW-DESIGN CHAIR COMPANY

Charlie, a young inventor, has just built a new folding chair with a design far superior to that of any other chair available. Because it is unique, Charlie decides to patent the design so that no one else can copy it. After receiving his patent, Charlie has several choices. He wants to get his chair manufactured so that consumers can buy it. And he wants to profit—make money—from his work.

One possibility for Charlie is to sell his patent to a chair-making company, which would probably pay him a large sum of money for it. The chair company would make the chair, and Charlie would not have to worry about it any longer. But Charlie believes that if he were to manufacture and sell the chairs himself, he could potentially make much more money than if he simply sold the design to a chair company. Encouraged by family and friends, he decides to turn his hobby of designing chairs into a full-time business. He will manufacture the chairs himself.

Charlie estimates that if he could make and sell at least 100,000 chairs a year, it would cost him about $20 to produce each chair. The $20 cost per chair would include what are called the *direct costs* of manufacturing: the supplies—steel, wood, screws, glue, and bolts—and wages for the workers in his factory. In addition, Charlie would have to pay people to sell his chairs to stores around the country (sales costs) and pay for advertising to make people aware of his chair's superior design.

Expenses for sales and advertising are known as *indirect costs*. Charlie estimates that these indirect costs would add up to about $10 per chair. Therefore, the total cost of each chair would be $30. He estimates that he could probably sell his chairs to dealers for $35 each.

In order to manufacture and sell 100,000 chairs, Charlie will also require a factory site, machinery, offices and office equipment, and corporate officers. If he is required to deliver his merchandise, Charlie will also need a fleet of trucks. These items would be known as the company's *assets*. The more chairs Charlie can produce using these assets, the more money he will make on each chair. Ac-

ONE CHAIR		100,000 CHAIRS	
Selling Price	$35.00	**Total Sales**	$3,500,000
Less Cost of Wood and Materials, Salaries, Labor, Other Direct Costs	20.00	Less Cost of Wood and Materials, Salaries, Labor, Other Direct Costs	2,000,000
Gross Profit	$15.00	**Gross Profit**	$1,500,000
Less Advertising Expenses, Sales Commissions, Other Expenses	10.00	Less Advertising Expenses, Sales Commissions, Other Expenses	1,000,000
Profit Before Taxes	$ 5.00	**Profit Before Taxes**	$ 500,000
		Less Federal, State, Local Taxes	240,000
		Net Profit or Earnings	$ 260,000

cording to Charlie's figures, his total start-up costs will be approximately $2 million.

Charlie believes his new enterprise would be beneficial in several ways. Thousands of people would prefer the new chairs because of their better design. Many workers in his community would earn a living by making and selling the chairs. The business would thus contribute to the welfare of his community, state, and country by employing these workers and by paying taxes. If Charlie could indeed manufacture and sell 100,000 chairs, this activity would no longer be a hobby. It would become a sizable business.

Raising Money for a New Business

Charlie now faces a major problem: Where will he get the $2 million he needs to start his company? His savings add up to about $10,000, not nearly enough. If he asked his family and friends to lend him money, he might be able to gather together an additional $15,000 or $20,000. But that is still far from the $2 million he needs.

Charlie might be able to borrow the money from a bank. Banks are in business to make loans to individuals and businesses. They lend a fixed amount of money for a set period of time that ranges from a couple of days to as long as several years. At the end of the loan period, the bank requires that the business repay the loan. In the meantime the bank charges a yearly fee called *interest*, which is figured as a percentage of the loan. However, Charlie will have a difficult time borrowing money from a bank. When banks lend money, they try to be sure the borrower will be able to pay the interest charge as well as the full amount of the loan, called the *principal*, within the specified times. To be certain they get their money back, banks often require borrowers to pledge some possessions of value. Such pledged valuables are called *collateral*. Collateral may consist of cars, houses, or other property that the bank can take over and sell to get its money back if a borrower does not repay a loan. But Charlie has no collateral. The only thing he owns is his patent for the new chair.

Charlie decides to find individuals, frequently called *venture capitalists*, who would be willing to provide money to start his business. Venture capitalists typically have large amounts of money that they use for this purpose. They are

willing to make risky investments, such as taking chances on young inventors like Charlie who have nothing more than an idea. If Charlie's business fails, the venture capitalists can lose most or all of their money. But they are willing to take a risk because they may make a substantial profit should the business prove successful. For this reason, the venture capitalists usually try to own a large part of the business in exchange for the use of their money. Then, if and when the business begins to make money, they will be able to share in the profits in proportion to their investment. A larger investment will yield greater profit. If the business is very successful, the venture capitalists can sell their part of the business to someone else and make an even larger profit on their initial investment.

Charlie decides that the best way to raise the capital to start his business is to interest these investors. He offers to divide his new business into smaller pieces in order to attract several investors as co-owners. Charlie realizes that if he gives part ownership of his business to the venture capitalists, he will no longer be entitled to all the profits. He will have to share the profits with others. However, he is willing to do this because he realizes that he would not be able to start his business at all without their help.

Charlie is introduced to several venture capitalists, who agree to give Charlie the money he needs in exchange for shared ownership of the company. The $2 million that Charlie has to start the business is called *equity capital.*

Equity refers to the property of a company, and equity capital is used to acquire property for a new or expanding company.

FORMING A CORPORATION

C harlie now has to decide which legal form his new business should take. He knows that businesses can be set up in a number of different legal forms. Each form has different characteristics. Some are taxed by the government more than others. Some allow one or two people to act as the sole owners of the business, whereas other forms enable many groups of people to be co-owners. After exploring the advantages and disadvantages of the various forms, he decides to establish a corporation. A corporation may be owned by many people. The principal reason he chooses this form is because corporations offer limited *financial liability*. This means that Charlie would not personally be responsible, or liable, if the company failed. Charlie has learned that no matter which legal structure he uses, any creditors (people or other companies to which his corporation owed money) would have first claim on his assets. That means that he would have to sell his business's assets (the factory, machinery, and so on) in order to pay these debts. In a corporation, the financial risk of the owners is limited to the amounts of money that they originally invested. For example, if Charlie's business failed while owing money, such as wages for his workers, Charlie would not be personally responsible for paying the entire debt. He would, though, like the other stockholders, be liable for the amount of his original investment.

BECOMING A STOCKHOLDER

Charlie forms the corporation in accordance with the laws of the state and names it "New-Design Chair Company." He and the venture capitalists become stockholders in the new company. Ownership of a corporation is divided into shares of stock. Each stockholder owns a part of the company proportionate to the amount of money she or he has invested and the number of shares of stock she or he owns.

Charlie selects a few people whose judgment he trusts to act as the board of directors until a permanent board is chosen at the first annual meeting of the company's stockholders. In a corporation, the board of directors is responsible for overseeing the affairs of the company. The board

is very important to a new company because its directors select the people who will actually run the business. Together they must decide who is elected to the board of directors. The stockholders will also make other decisions about the company at the first meeting.

When the New-Design Chair Company was incorporated, its charter authorized it to create 400,000 shares of stock and hold them for the company's use. These shares have no value at first; they are merely available for the company to sell, or issue, when it decides that the time is right. Four hundred thousand shares were determined to be a convenient and practical amount for the company's needs.

At its first meeting, the board of directors votes to issue 250,000 shares of the 400,000 total. These shares are divided among Charlie and the investors accord-ing to the proportion of the company they own. The extent of their ownership depends primarily on how much money they invested. The venture capitalists who invested the most money will be given the greatest amount of shares. However, because Charlie designed the chair and owns the patent on it, and because of his importance in running the company, he will get a large number of shares without having invested as much as the venture capitalists. As it turns out, Charlie ends up owning 100,000 shares of stock, or 40 percent of the company. The remaining 150,000 shares are divided among the venture capitalists in pro-portion to their individual investments. Charlie and the venture capitalists are now referred to as "stockholders in common" or "common stockholders." The shares they own are known as *common stock*.

Each stockholder is a part owner in the company, al-though how much of the company each owns depends on the number of shares held. Charlie owns 2/5 of the com-pany; someone who holds 50,000 shares of the total 250,000 owns 1/5; and a person with only 50 shares owns 1/5000 of the entire company. The 150,000 shares that were author-ized but not issued may be sold by the directors at a later date.

At the present time, there are 250,000 shares of stock outstanding, or issued and owned. When it comes time for the stockholders to elect the board of directors or vote on other matters, each share outstanding is entitled to an equal vote. Each shareholder has as many votes as he or she has shares of stock.

When the Company Needs More Money

A few months after it starts operations, the New-Design Chair Company begins to plan for the future. Sales are promising already, so Charlie and his board of directors decide to expand and manufacture more chairs next year. To do this, the company will need more than the original $2 million from the venture capitalists. To get this additional money, the company decides to go into debt. It will borrow the money and pay it back later with the money received from the sale of newly manufactured chairs. Because the company expects to repay this money in a relatively short period of time, it can go to a bank for a loan. Now that the company is formally established and worth at least $2 million, it is quite likely that a bank would be willing to lend it money.

If the business were better established, with a proven history of good performance, it might consider raising money by selling bonds to the public. This would be a good way to raise money if the company expected to need a longer amount of time before repaying the debt. Bonds are similar to bank loans: In exchange for the privilege of borrowing money, the company agrees to pay the lenders a set interest rate each year for a fixed period of time. At the end of that time, say, ten years, the company will repay the full amount, or principal, of the loan.

Charlie then finds a bank that will lend money to the New-Design Chair Company. The bank requires New-Design to put up some of its property as collateral. If the debt is not repaid as promised, the property pledged as collateral will be sold by the bank to replace the money that was borrowed.

Whether it gets money from a bank or from bondholders, the New-Design Chair Company will have to pay interest on the money it borrows. However, it will not have to issue any more stock to obtain the extra money. This is very important to the current stockholders. If the company issued more stock in exchange for this money, the stockholders would have to give up some of their ownership of the company, just as Charlie did when he gave up some of his ownership to the venture capitalists in exchange for their original $2 million investment. (The company could have raised money by issuing stock, using the 150,000 authorized shares that were not issued originally.) On the other hand, the lenders—bank or bondholders—would have first claim on the company's property if the company failed to repay its debt (called a "default").

Organizing the Company

Every company consists of a number of employees who perform different tasks essential to the operation of the business, and the New-Design Chair Company is no ex-

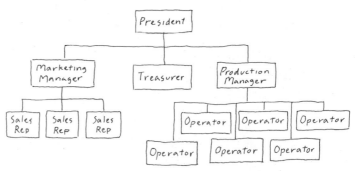

Organization Chart
for the NEW-DESIGN CHAIR COMPANY

ception. In manufacturing firms like Charlie's, most of the people employed by the company work with the equipment that is directly involved with production, that is, making the product. A smaller number of people who work in the organization are managers, and most of them do not work on the factory floor. They are responsible for making decisions about important matters regarding the company's operations and supervising other workers.

Charlie's staff of managers was small at first, but it grew as the business expanded. The initial key managers included the president (Charlie), who managed the company's activities and coordinated the efforts of others, and a treasurer, who supervised financial matters.

In any organization, the president (sometimes called the chief executive officer, or CEO) is responsible for overseeing the day-to-day activities of the company and coordinating the efforts of the other employees. The president makes the vital decisions regarding the future of the company and reports to the board of directors.

The treasurer (sometimes called the chief financial officer) oversees all of the company's financial matters. Large and small businesses alike must keep track of a vast number of bills, checks, and bank accounts. They must monitor how much they spend and the amounts they owe to banks, employees, and suppliers from whom they buy equipment and materials. They must also know how much money they are owed by the businesses that buy from them. The treasurer also monitors the taxes owed by the company to local, state, and federal govern-
ments. The treasurer is re-
sponsible for keeping track
of all this financial information and making deci-
sions regarding the
amount of money the com-

pany can spend or how much it must borrow in order to continue operating on a day-to-day basis.

Charlie hired two other managers almost immediately: a marketing manager to direct the company's salespeople and selling efforts, and a production manager who is responsible for the actual process of manufacturing the New-Design chairs.

The marketing manager is responsible for making potential buyers aware of the chairs and then selling to them. Charlie's chair is terrific, but if people don't know about it or it isn't available in stores, no one will buy it. The marketing manager must train the salespeople or representatives ("reps"), who then go out to convince the owners of furniture stores that the chairs are indeed superior to other folding chairs and that they should carry them in their stores. The marketing manager will tell the sales reps about the extensive advertising campaign the company is planning in order to make the public aware of the superior qualities of the New-Design chairs. Once the chairs are in the stores, they will probably sell well.

The production manager is responsible for the actual manufacture of the chairs. He must oversee the entire production process, from the time that the unfinished metal, screws, wood, and other materials are delivered to the factory until the chairs are completed and ready to send out. He must make sure that the machines and the employees who run the machines are working efficiently and effectively. He is responsible for hiring the production workers to make the chairs and for supervising them so that they do their jobs well.

Charlie also has several people outside the company who advise him about specific problems. Among these advisers are his banker, his attorney, and his accountant.

The banker assisted the company in borrowing money from the bank when it needed it. The attorney advised Charlie on legal issues that concerned the company, such as the advantages of being a corporation. Periodically, the accountant puts the company's records into a standard form, a financial statement, that Charlie, the board of directors, the treasurer, and the banker can refer to. They all want to know how the company is doing. Is it making money, losing money, or breaking even? All these advisers were consulted from time to time as the New-Design Chair Company encountered the many problems that most new companies face on a daily basis. Charlie found the independent advice from these people especially helpful during the first several months of operations, when he and his management team were learning to run a business together and gaining their operating experience.

Charlie learned many lessons about running a business in the early days of his company. One of the most important concerned the role of marketing. *Marketing* refers to all efforts used to make prospective customers aware of the company's product. If people do not know about a product, they are unable to buy it. New-Design had to work hard to promote and advertise its superior chairs to the public. Charlie remembered that, in the business course he had taken a few years earlier, the professor stressed the contribution of marketing to the success of any company. Now Charlie worked closely with his marketing manager to plan ways of telling people about the new chairs.

THE IMPORTANCE OF PROFITS

Why did Charlie and his associates risk their personal savings to build a factory to manufacture chairs? They could have put their money into a savings bank rather than into the new enterprise. The money would have been safe, and the bank would have paid them interest. Why would anyone be willing to risk money—let alone $2 million—to start the New-Design Chair Company? The answer is simple: profits.

A company makes profits when the total amount of money it receives is greater than the total amount of money it spends. A company receives money by selling its products or services. It spends money on its buildings or offices, equipment, materials, and labor. The New-Design Chair Company, for example, received $3,500,000 for the sale of chairs in its first year. To make those chairs, it spent a total of $3,240,000. Therefore its profit was $260,000. A loss is the opposite of profits. A loss results when the costs are greater than the receipts.

Charlie and his associates saw an opportunity to make a profit on each chair they could manufacture and sell to the public. Even more important, they saw the possibility of increasing their profits in later years by manufacturing and selling more chairs. For this reason, Charlie and his investors estimated that by investing in the new company they could make much more money by leaving their money in the bank and earning interest.

Now time has passed. Charlie's projections were accurate, and the venture has been successful. The New-Design Chair Company sold 100,000 chairs in its first year, resulting in a *net profit*, also called *earnings*, of $260,000, just as Charlie had anticipated. The net profit is the profit a company realizes after all expenses, costs, and taxes have been paid. This infor-

mation is sent to all the stockholders in the annual report of the company. The annual report describes the company's work and its financial performance for the year. A table known as an *income statement* or *P & L* (profit and loss) details the company's expenses and earnings over the course of a single year. Another table in the annual report, the *balance sheet*, details the company's present financial condition, including how much it owns (what its assets are worth) and how much it owes (what its liabilities are).

Distributing the Profits

What should New-Design do with its net profit of $260,000? Deciding what to do with profits is one of the toughest decisions a company must make. Because the stockholders are the owners of the company, they are entitled to divide this money among themselves. Considering that there are 250,000 shares outstanding, dividing the earnings of $260,000 equally means that a stockholder would be entitled to $1.04 for every share held ($260,000 divided by 250,000 shares). This calculation is called *earnings per share*. If, next year or the year after, the New-

Design Chair Company increases its production of chairs and earns, for example, $500,000, the earnings per share would be $2 ($500,000 divided by 250,000 shares).

Each year the board of directors of the company must decide what to do with these profits. The directors have several choices. They could distribute all or part of last year's $260,000 earnings to the shareholders in the form of an equal payment for each share of stock. This payment is known as a *dividend*. Companies usually pay dividends to shareholders by check every three months, or four times a year (quarterly). The amount of the dividend can vary, but it is usually determined by the amount of profits the company has earned. (A company would not want to distribute dividends if it did not make a profit.) When dividends are sent to stockholders, an equal amount of money is paid for each share of common stock. For that reason, the stockholder owning the greatest number of shares would, of course, receive the largest dividend check.

Companies usually don't distribute all of their profits to the shareholders in the form of a dividend. To do so would leave no money for the company's own use. For this reason, the directors of the New-Design Chair Company might decide to declare only a small dividend or perhaps none at all in the first year. They could then use the year's profits to increase the size of the factory, buy more machines, hire more workers, or add to the company's research program to design even better chairs. That is, they would reinvest the profits into the company. Profits that are reinvested are known as *retained earnings*.

By reinvesting the earnings instead of distributing them to the shareholders, the company could expand without borrowing more money from banks or other investors. This process is called *internal financing* because money for running and expanding comes from within the company and not from outside sources. Reinvestment might enable the company to produce more chairs and thereby increase profits in future years. The stockholders would then enjoy higher dividends, and New-Design will indeed have been a good investment for them.

As it turns out, at the next meeting of the board of New-Design, the directors declare a dividend of $.26 per share, or a total of $65,000. This is one fourth of the earnings. The $.26 per share is a *payout* of 25 percent of the $1.04 total earnings per share ($1.04 × .25 = .26). The remaining $195,000 of profits can then be spent to expand the business.

The retained earnings will also enhance the company's financial condition. By reinvesting most of the profits back into the business, the owners of the New-Design Chair Company will add to its assets in the form of machinery, factory space, or other property that helps increase chair production. Because retained earnings are very similar to an investment in the company, they increase the stockholders' equity, or value of that part of the company owned by the stockholders. In the balance sheet printed in the company's annual report, the stockholders' equity is shown as a component of assets. When investors look at a balance sheet, they prefer to see a company that has more assets than liabilities.

Measuring Profitability

Stockholders of the New-Design Chair Company will be watching the company's earnings very closely. They hope that its profits will grow each year. This would be a sign that the company is successful and should be able to expand even more and become even more profitable. When they examine the company's profitability, they will be asking two basic questions:

- How much profit is produced by each dollar of sales? Return on revenues, expressed as a percentage, is an important measure of the company's efficiency. It is calculated by dividing net profit by total revenues. For the New-Design Chair Company, profits are 7.4 percent of revenues ($260,000 ÷ $3,500,000 = .074 = 7.4%). This means that every dollar of sales included 7.4 cents profit. The greater profit a company can produce from each dollar of sales the better.

- How much profit is produced by each dollar of stockholders' equity? Originally, stockholders' equity consisted of the $2 million investment made by Charlie and the venture capitalists. Each year the stockholders will want to see how well their investment is doing. Profitability is calculated by dividing the year's profits by the stockholders' equity ($260,000 ÷ $2,000,000 = .13 = 13%), which means that every dollar of original investment produced $.13 in profit. This is expressed as 13 percent return on equity (ROE).

A typical company in the United States earns 5 percent ROE from total sales in a year. In other words, for every dollar of sales, a company earns 5 cents profit. This same amount of profit represents approximately 13 to 14 percent profit for every dollar invested in a company. By these

Earnings (net profit)	Total Revenues	Return on Revenue: Profit per Dollar of Sales*	Stockholders' Equity	Return on Equity: Profit per Dollar of Investment**
$260,000	$3,500,000	$ .074 (7.4%)	$2,000,000	$ .13 (13%)

*Earnings divided by revenue.   **Earnings divided by total investment (equity).*

measures, the New-Design Chair Company is doing quite well in its first year.

Profits are important to everyone in our economic system. The opportunity to make a profit encourages people to start a business, invest their money (and the money of others) in that business, and devote their energies to making it successful. They hope to make profits in the future and earn money for themselves and others. If they can create a product such as Charlie's new chair, then they are free to go ahead and try to do so. The opportunity to make profits spurs people on to start and invest in businesses, build factories, open stores, make better products, offer needed services, and create jobs for workers. A profitable business keeps workers employed, provides goods and services that people want, pays taxes, and in these and other ways adds to the well-being of the community.

(continued on page 32)

REAL LIFE: SELLING NIKE

Nike, the athletic shoe company, was established as a small gym- and running-shoe manufacturer in Beaverton, Oregon, in 1969. Today it is the largest manufacturer of jogging shoes in the country. In the early 1970s, founder and owner Philip Knight noticed that jogging was becoming increasingly popular. He began designing and manufacturing running shoes that were particularly suited to the requirements of the everyday runner. They were light, well padded, and comfortable on pavement or concrete.

Demand for the new shoe skyrocketed. Everybody wanted a pair of Nike running shoes, and not just for running. People took to wearing their Nikes for everyday walking as well. In no time at all, the company was selling millions of pairs of running shoes—compared with only a few hundred thousand pairs a few years before. To meet the increased demand, Nike had to expand its manufacturing facilities and find sources of money to pay for the expansion.

Many investors around the country had heard about the company's success and were eager to buy its stock. They had seen the rapid growth in popularity of Nike shoes in their own homes. It seemed certain that the company would have a bright and very profitable future.

Selected Financial Data NIKE, INC.	1986	1985	1981
	(in thousands, except for share data)		
Year Ended May 31:			
Revenues	$1,069,222	$946,371	$457,742
Net income	59,211	10,270	25,955
Net income per common share	1.55	.27	.76
Cash dividends declared per common share	.40	.40	—
At May 31:			
Total assets	$ 476,838	$503,966	$230,289
Common shareholders' equity	316,846	271,668	83,021

Nike's stock was issued to the public on December 2, 1980, at $22 a share. The price was high compared with that of most shoe company stocks. After a couple of months, the stock price fell slightly to $18 for no apparent reason. Some professionals thought the original offering price of the stock had been too high. But a few months later, the price recovered to $20, and by July 1981 it was up to $23. After eight months, Nike announced that it could forecast even higher earnings for the year than it had targeted. This bolstered investors' confidence, and in December, one year after the stock was issued, the share price had climbed to $28. Investors who sold after holding the stock for a single year made $6 on every share. The return on their investment would have been equal to $6/$28, or 21 percent (6 ÷ 28 = .21).

As other shoe manufacturers began to realize how profitable running shoes could be, they began to compete with Nike. By 1984, the increased competition in the running- and sport-shoe market had slowed down Nike's earnings and growth. The stock price began to decline, until it reached a low of less than $7 in 1985. The following year, though, the company introduced some new products, trimmed expenses, and improved total sales. Stock prices responded, reaching a high for the year of almost $19 in 1986. At the close of the 1986 financial year, there were 6,500 shareholders, and they received dividends of $.40 per share. On the cover of its annual report, Nike boasted of "a record year." Total revenues topped $1 billion, and net income per share was six times that of the previous year.

THE STOCK PRICE

W hen a company issues stock, how is the price determined? There is an old Wall Street saying: "A stock is worth only what someone is willing to pay for it." Although the saying does not tell the whole story, there is some truth to it. Stocks do not have a set or predetermined value. The company has no document that says its stock is worth, say, $4 and not more or less. Stockholders who want to sell their shares in the New-Design Chair Company, for example, could sell for no more than the price someone else was willing to pay. Stocks are seldom sold back to the company that issued them, since the company's financial resources are tied up in its regular business activities.

The price of a share of stock is determined in an open marketplace—the stock market—by large groups of buyers and sellers. Although there can be millions of buyers and sellers in these marketplaces each day, the process that goes on between buyer and seller is fairly simple. On one side of the transaction is someone trying to sell a stock for a certain price. On the other side of the transaction is someone trying to buy that stock. The final price of the stock is the price at which the seller agrees to sell and the buyer agrees to buy.

Typically, a particularly attractive stock will cost more than a share of stock that no one wants. For example, if a company is prospering and the outlook for its future is bright, there could be many investors so eager to own its stock that they might be willing to pay a fairly high price to get it. Doing so would create a great demand for the company's stock. Anyone selling the stock would be able to sell it for a high price. Most of the people who already own the stock, knowing the company's future is bright, would probably want to keep it, so the number of shares of stock available to be sold would be small. The price of the stock would then rise until it reached a point at which the people who owned the stock would be willing to sell it to those who wanted to buy it. Some people owning the attractive stock would decide they can make a good profit by selling at this high price, since the price at which they had bought the stock was substantially lower. The price responds to the law of supply and demand. The higher the demand for something, the more limited the supply and the more people are willing to pay for it. If the price goes too high, the buyers would not be interested in buying. If the price stays too low, the sellers would not be interested in selling.

On the other hand, if the outlook for a company is unfavorable and its earnings prospects are dim, then eager buyers may be very scarce. At the same time, those stock-holders who feel that there is too little chance of making a profit, might want to sell in order to invest their money elsewhere. The only way to attract buyers in such a high-supply, low-demand situation would be to reduce the price of the stock. Here again, the law of supply and demand would dictate the price of the stock.

WHAT INVESTORS MUST CONSIDER

How can an investor buying or selling a stock judge the current value of that stock? Investors must constantly estimate what they think a share of stock is worth. There are many different factors investors can consider. They must keep in mind that because each share of stock represents a part of a company, the value of the stock will reflect the value of the company. For this reason, most investors want to get a sense of the value of the company. Three key factors—a company's earnings outlook, its dividend prospects, and its overall financial condition—help investors compare a particular stock to other investment opportunities.

- *Earnings outlook* is a forecast of how much profit a company is likely to make in the future. Investors want to buy stock in companies that are likely to become more profitable. Investors who are concerned about the growth of their investment are particularly interested in the earnings outlook.

- *Dividend prospects* are the amount of earnings that the company distributes to stockholders each year. As we saw in the case of the New-Design Chair Company, the size of the dividend was an important issue for the board of directors to resolve. Investors who are concerned about receiving regular income from their investment are particularly interested in the dividend prospects. A company that has good dividend prospects can expect to send its stockholders a dividend payout by check every three months.

- *Financial condition* describes what a company owns and  what it owes to other people, and it is an important index of how much a company is worth. Investors are not attracted to companies that own few assets and have high liabilities. They want to buy stock in a financially healthy, well-run company. What a company owns and owes is shown in its financial statements.

The price of a stock is influenced by these three fundamental factors. But over a period of days, weeks, or months, the price of a stock can fluctuate widely. The price may depend on factors affecting the company or its industry, the overall direction of the stock market at a particular time, or on events or news items affecting the company, industry, stock market, or national economy. Sometimes a stock's price will rise and fall for no apparent reason. Any number of circumstances or events can influence the confidence levels of investors and the balance of supply and demand between buyers and sellers. Over an extended time period—a few years or longer—a stock price will most likely rise or fall as the company's earnings and dividends increase or decrease and as its financial condition appears healthy or poor.

How do investors determine how much they are willing to pay for a stock or at what price they want to sell a stock? They may take a value approach, comparing the current price of a stock that interests them to that of other companies in the same industry. Does the stock increase in price when others in the same business do? Does it lead the pack or lag behind? An investor might research a company and an industry for several weeks or months to learn about its present value and potential success. No two investors will agree entirely on how to decide how much a stock is worth.

To actually evaluate these factors in dollars-and-cents terms, investors use two ways to analyze stocks: price/earnings ratio and dividend yield.

P/E Ratio   The *price/earnings ratio* (P/E ratio or P/E multiple) describes the relationship between the stock price and the company's earnings per share. For a stock whose price is $30 and annual earnings are $1.50 per share, the P/E ratio is 30/1.50 (read as "thirty to one fifty"). The P/E ratio can also be expressed as a multiple. To determine the multiple equivalent of a ratio, reduce the ratio fraction to lowest terms: Simply divide the price of the stock by the earnings per share ($30 ÷ $1.50 = 20). This means that the cost of a share of stock is 20 times the amount of earnings per share.

The P/E ratio gives investors a standard, relatively simple way to relate the price of a stock to its earnings performance. An investor can evaluate stocks by comparing their P/E ratios. Is a stock overpriced if it has a P/E ratio of 20? Is it an exceptional value with a P/E ratio of 10? The higher the P/E ratio of a stock, the more an investor pays for that stock's earnings per share. The lower the P/E ratio, the less the investor pays for that company's earnings per share.

The P/E ratio also provides a standard way to compare two or more stocks. How can an investor decide which stock to buy when the prices and earnings per share of two stocks are completely different? The P/E ratios are a rough guide to whether one stock is cheaper than the other. For example, suppose the stock of record company A is selling for $30, whereas record company B's stock is selling for $20. Their earnings per share are $3 and $1, respectively. What are the P/E ratios of the two stocks? A's P/E ratio is 10 (30 ÷ 3); B's is 20 (20 ÷ 1). Which is more expensive? Company A's stock certainly costs more, but it has a lower P/E ratio than company B's stock. It could be said that company's B's stock is actually more expensive.

Many investors look for stocks that have low P/E ratios. They see the ratio as an indicator that the stock is cheap in comparison to other stocks. However, it is a mistake to assume than a stock having a low P/E ratio is automatically more attractively priced than another stock having a higher P/E. A stock with a P/E ratio of 8, for example, is not necessarily a better value than one with a ratio of 15. Is there reason to think that the earnings of the second company will grow rapidly in the future? If so, investors will be willing to buy the stock at the higher P/E ratio.

Dividend Yield   The *dividend yield*, often referred to simply as *yield*, describes what percentage of a stock's price is paid out to investors in a cash distribution each year. The yield of a stock is calculated by dividing the annual cash dividend per share by the price of the stock. In the case of a stock priced at $30 per share, the dividend per share may be 60 cents. The yield is then 60 cents divided by 30, or .02, or 2 percent. Investors can evaluate stocks by comparing their dividend yield. Stocks that pay a higher dividend yield are paying out more cash to the investor than stocks with lower yields.

It would be a mistake, though, to assume that stocks that pay a high dividend yield are more attractive than stocks with lower yields. There are other factors for investors to consider. How safe or secure is the dividend? Is the dividend of the low-yield stock likely to be increased next year? Is the dividend low because the company has reinvested a large part of its earnings and is thus on the verge of expansion? How does the yield compare with that of other companies in the same industry? Is a company with higher yields depriving itself of money that it could use to expand its factories or research and development efforts?

Neither the P/E ratio nor the dividend yield remain constant. When a stock price goes up, the P/E ratio increases and the dividend yield declines. Conversely, when the stock price goes down, the P/E ratio declines and the dividend yield increases. Moreover, the P/E ratio and dividend yield will also vary as the company's earnings and dividends increase or decrease.

(continued on page 40)

BECOME A PAPER INVESTOR

A good way to learn about the stock market is to become a "paper investor." Paper investors do not use real money in the stock market. Instead, they pretend to invest a certain amount of money, perhaps $100, in a single stock or group of stocks, and they follow their stocks' performance over a period of time to see whether they would have made or lost money.

The first step in becoming a paper investor is to choose a stock or group of stocks that interests you. The first place to look for good stocks is in your own home. What products do you use every day? Think of everything from sneakers and breakfast cereals to batteries and cars. Shares of many of the companies that make these products are traded in the stock market. For instance, Nike, Mattel, McDonald's, Coca-Cola, and Quaker Oats each have millions of shares of stock that are traded. When you choose a product you know about, you have an interest in it and some sense of how popular or successful it is. This can be a clue as to how well the stock could do in the future. For example, what soft drink do your friends prefer? What brands of electronic equipment, cameras, or computers are used by the people you know? In your neighborhood do you see more new cars made by Ford than by General Motors?

After you have selected the products you are most interested in, find out the names of the companies that make them. Not all products are sold under the name of the parent company. Minute Maid orange juice, for instance, is a Coca-Cola product. You may have to read the small print on the package or box to find the name of the parent company. It is possible that some of the companies you choose cannot be tracked down in the papers. They may still be "privately" owned and might not have issued stock to the public.

The next step is to find out at what price your company's stock is selling. Most daily newspapers in the United States have a business section that lists almost all of the names and daily prices of publicly traded stock. Find the names of your companies in the stock listings; they will be listed alphabetically. The name of your company may be abbreviated to save space. For instance, General Electric, the company that manufactures light bulbs, among other products, is listed as "GenEl." Eastman Kodak is listed as "EKodk." To find your company's stock prices, you will probably have to look through listings for the three major stock markets: the New York Stock Exchange for most of the largest companies; the American Stock Exchange for medium-sized companies; and the NASDAQ (National Association of Securities Dealers Automated Quotations)

Over-the-Counter Quotations for the smaller and youngest companies.

When you locate the name of a company on one of these listings, you will find a row of numbers set up in columns to the right of the name. The most important column is the second one from the far right. It bears the heading "Last." The number listed for your company is the last price your stock sold for in the stock market at the market "close" at the end of the previous business day. (For more information about stock listings, see *Reading the Financial Pages*, another volume in the *Basic Investor's Library*.)

| 52-Week | | | | Sales | | | | |
High	Low	Stock	Div	100s	High	Low	Last	Chg.
17½	8	Hracct		90	17¼	16¾	17	+ ⅛
45½	22	MyStck	.40	1360	45½	44½	45½	+ 2¼
30	21¼	Yrbank		13	29½	28¾	29½	...

How many shares of this stock can you buy with your imaginary money? Divide the amount you plan to "invest" by the price of the stock listed to see how many shares you can own. (It may be a fraction.) Suppose you plan to invest $100 on paper and choose a stock that sold yesterday for 21⅝. That means each share of stock cost $21.63. You will be able to "buy" 4⅗ shares (100 ÷ 21.63 = 4.6).

Write down the number of shares you own, the price of the stock, and the date. The next day, look at the listings and check the new price. The last column in the stock listings, headed "Chg." (net change), will immediately tell you how much the stock's price has gone up or down from the day before.

Keep a log of your stocks' daily prices for a month or longer to see how your stocks do over that time period. In the end, did they go up or down in price? Are you "richer" or "poorer" on paper?

A good way to see a stock's general movement over a period of time is to plot its price on a graph. Write the dates of the business days (days when the stock markets are open; the markets are closed on weekends and most holidays) of the month on the horizontal axis of the graph and a range of prices for the stock on the vertical axis. Each day mark with a dot the price of the stock next to the appropriate numeral. Then connect the dots with a line. At the end of the month, a glance will tell you how your stock performed.

WHY DO PEOPLE BUY STOCKS?

People buy stocks because they want to make money. When people have money that they don't need for living expenses, they want not only to keep their money safe but to use it to make more money. Most people do not simply put extra money in the cookie jar or under the mattress. Should they put it in a savings bank? Buy government bonds? Invest in real estate or objects of art? Or should they turn to the stock market? If money is not invested, it will just sit in the cookie jar and not earn anything at all. In a savings account at a bank, the money will earn a relatively small amount of interest each year, but it can be taken out when needed. If the person buys land or a piece of art, the value may increase over time, but the investor would have to sell the land or painting to get the money. There are no interest or dividend payments, and the value of some land and art objects may decrease. In the stock market, investors hope to buy a stock and sell it for a higher price later, collecting dividends on the investment in the meantime. Investors put their extra money to work to make more money.

If a stock increases in price, the stockholder makes money only by selling the stock. An increase in the value of a stock is known as *capital appreciation*. Until the stock is sold, the investor's profit or loss as the stock's price moves higher or lower than the original purchase price is called a *paper profit* or *paper loss*. The investor can calculate the losses or gains as often as desired by using pencil and paper or a calculator. But the actual profit or loss is not realized until the investor sells the stock.

For example, suppose you bought a share of stock for $10. For the next five days the price of the stock stays at $10. Then, on the sixth day, the company holds a news conference and announces that its sales have increased 25 percent. This probably means that profits will go up, too. Now more people want to own the stock. As a result of this increased demand, the price moves up to $15. You have made a "paper" profit of $5. The next day some of the excitement among the investors wears off and the price drops to $14. You decide to sell at that price. At that point you realize (actually receive) a profit of $4, $1 less than your paper profit of the day before.

Perspectives on Buying Stock

There are basically three ways in which an individual can participate in the stock market: investing, speculating, and trading.

- *Long-term investing* is generally one of the most successful approaches, because time can be used to advantage. An investor buys shares for a long period of time, perhaps two years or longer, and becomes a part owner of a company. Investors believe that the company will prosper over time and, through dividends and increases in stock value, provide at least an adequate return on their investment. They choose a company in which they have confidence. As the company prospers, the stock's price should increase at least enough to offset any increase in the cost of living (inflation). Investors do not mind waiting out a temporary decline in the price of a stock because they are confident that over the long haul it will rise.

- *Speculating* implies a willingness to assume great risk for a potentially great reward. Being part owner of a company is not important to speculators. They buy stock in order to make money on it as quickly as possible. They may buy the stock of a very small or offbeat company because they think there is a chance that the  stock's price will rise sharply. Speculators may depend more on tips and rumors than on comparative figures. They try to score a hit when the price of a stock suddenly rises. But they may tie their money up in a company that goes nowhere for a long time.

- *Trading* is the frequent buying and selling of stocks. A  trader attempts to take advantage of small price changes in the stock and is less interested in the overall value of the company. Stock certificates are considered merely pieces of paper to be bought or sold for a profit within a short period of time—sometimes days or even hours. To be successful, traders must constantly monitor the prices of their stocks. If they think that a stock is going to increase in price by even 50 cents, they will buy it, wait for it to rise, and then sell it immediately. Traders usually buy very large numbers of shares of a single stock so that a small increase will be multiplied over many shares of stock when they choose to sell.

People in different situations and at different stages of life may have different investment goals. A person who is retired and needs additional cash for living expenses, for example, might invest with the goal of obtaining fairly secure regular income from dividends. A younger person who has an adequate current income and is looking to the future, might invest with an objective of growth and a modest dividend return. A person who has other sources of income might not be concerned about current dividend return but might be willing to assume greater risk for a potentially greater future return. This person might buy shares of small, rapidly growing companies in the hope that their stock may increase in price dramatically over a few months or years.

Whatever the investor's situation, it is particularly important to put only as much money in the stock market as he or she can safely afford, to identify an investment objective, and to know what to expect from each dollar invested.

Owning stock is a way for everyone to participate in the nation's economic growth. Millions of people own stocks today, including many young people with small amounts of investment capital. People under the age of 18 years are legally minors, limited in many ways by the law. Although minors cannot buy stocks for themselves, they can legally own shares of stock by purchasing them through a so-called custodial account in which an adult acts as guardian. Many young people are given gifts of money, perhaps in the hope that it will be saved for future education. Investing is a way to make that money grow.

GLOSSARY

assets Everything that a company owns, including what is owed to it. Assets can include cash, equipment, or patents.

board of directors A group of people elected by a company's *stockholders* that determines the basic policy of the company.

bond A certificate that represents a loan to a company. The issuing company (the borrower) pays *interest* for the use of the money and must repay the entire amount of the bond at a specified time.

capital Money invested to create, or expand a business.

chief executive officer (CEO) The person responsible for directing and coordinating the overall activities of a company.

chief financial officer The person responsible for supervising the financial activities of a company.

collateral Valuable property that is used as security for a loan. If the borrower does not repay the loan, the collateral is forfeited to the lender.

corporation One of the legal forms in which a business can be established. The people who own the business are able to act as one; each is financially responsible only up to the amount he or she originally invested.

default Failure to fulfill obligations under a contract; usually the inability to pay money when due.

dividend A portion of a company's *earnings* that is distributed to *stockholders*; the amount is determined by the *board of directors*.

dividend yield The ratio of a company's current *dividend* to the current price of a *share of its stock*.

earnings, net earnings, or **net profit** A company's *revenues* minus its costs, expenses, and taxes, figured before paying dividends.

earnings per share A company's *net profit* divided by the number of *shares of stock* outstanding.

equity The net worth of a company; the value of a company's *assets* minus its *liabilities*.

financial statement A report showing the income, expenditures, *assets*, and *liabilities* of a company.

interest A periodic charge paid to a lender for the use of borrowed money.

internal financing The use of money from a company's *earnings* to operate or expand a business.

investment Property acquired for the purpose of gaining future income. Purchased stocks are an investment.

liabilities Debts, payments due to suppliers, salaries due to employees, and anything else that a company owes.

marketing The activities involved in selling a company's product or services to prospective customers.

NASDAQ (pronounced "nazdak") The computerized National Association of Securities Dealers Automatic Quotation network that provides price quotations on stocks and *bonds* traded only *over-the-counter*, that is, not listed on an exchange.

over-the-counter market The nationwide network of brokers/dealers who handle transactions of stocks and *bonds* that are not listed on an exchange.

44

payout The amount of *earnings* available for *dividends* that is actually paid to *stockholders*.

price/earnings ratios, P/E ratio The price of a *share of stock* divided by the *earnings per share*. The calculation is used to compare the cost of a stock to its earnings performance.

principal The original or total amount of a loan; the face value of a *bond*.

profit The amount of *earnings* remaining after a company pays all of its expenses.

retained earnings *Profits* that are kept by the company and not distributed to *stockholders* in the form of *dividends*.

return or *yield* The *interest* or *dividends* received from a loan or *investment*; can be expressed as a percentage of current price.

revenues All income received by a company as a result of its operations.

share of stock Any of the equal parts into which the entire value, or *equity*, of a company is divided. It represents part ownership in the company.

shares authorized The maximum number of stock shares that a company can issue according to its charter.

shares outstanding The number of *authorized shares* that have actually been issued and sold to investors.

stockholder, shareholder An owner of a *share* or *shares of stock* in a company.

supply and demand The relationship between the price, amount available, and demand for an item or service, including *shares of stock*. When demand is high and supply is low, people are willing to pay more.

venture capitalist An individual who provides money, known as "seed money," to start or expand a business and is willing to make a risky *investment* in the hope of making a large *profit*.

FURTHER READING

Consumer Reports, published by Consumer's Union. A monthly magazine featuring objective product comparisons; may be helpful for choosing stocks that have growth potential. Also contains financial advice and explanations.

Engel, Louis, and Brendan Boyd. *How to Buy Stocks*, 7th rev. ed. Boston: Little, Brown and Company, 1982. A classic on the subject; gives basic information about common stocks, over-the-counter stocks, and how stocks are bought and sold.

Finley, Harold M. *Everybody's Guide to the Stock Market*, 4th rev. ed. Chicago: Henry Regnery, 1968. An all-purpose guide to understanding the stock market; follows the progress of a fictitious company from its incorporation to its eventual public ownership.

Money, published by Time Inc. A monthly magazine dealing with a broad range of finance-related topics; includes basic articles for the beginning investor.

Shufro, Edward. *The New Investor's Guide to Wall Street*. New York: Lion Press, 1970. Describes how a company is formed and goes public; also gives tips on investing.

And a resource: New York Stock Exchange, Visitor's Center, 20 Broad Street, 3rd floor, New York, New York. Permanent exhibits; free tour includes a lecture, film, and gallery viewing of the trading floor. Advance reservations necessary for groups of more than ten.

INDEX

JEFFREY B. LITTLE, a finance graduate of New York University, began his Wall Street career in the early 1960s. He has worked as an accountant for a retail brokerage firm, as an instructor of technical analysis in a broker training center, as a securities analyst of technology stocks, and as a portfolio manager and advisory committee member for a major mutual fund. He is a Fellow of the Financial Analysts Federation, a member of the New York Society of Security Analysts, and was formerly a vice-president of an investment counsel firm in Baltimore.

PAUL A. SAMUELSON, senior editorial consultant, is Institute Professor Emeritus at the Massachusetts Institute of Technology. He is author (now coauthor) of the best-selling textbook *Economics*. He served as an adviser to President John F. Kennedy and in 1970 was the first American to win the Nobel Prize in economics.

SHAWN PATRICK BURKE, consulting editor, is a securities analyst with Standard & Poor's Corporation. He has been an internal consultant in industry as well as for a Wall Street investment firm, and he has extensive experience in computer-generated financial modeling and analysis.

ROBERT W. WRUBEL, contributing editor, is an associate editor with *Financial World* magazine and was previously associate financial editor with Boardroom Reports, Inc. A graduate of Yale University, he has been a financial analyst for a Wall Street securities firm and has written extensively on finance and investment topics.

ACKNOWLEDGMENTS Page 8, courtesy of the New York Stock Exchange; 11, 14, 16–18, 20–27, 34, 39, 41–42, illustrations by David Garner; 30, photograph by Ira N. Toff.

Cover: photograph by George Haling.